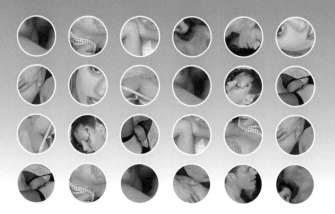

T0125794

EROTIC Dots

THIS IS A CARLTON BOOK

Text and Design copyright © Carlton Publishing Group 1999
Photography by John Mason

This edition published in 2013 by Carlton Books Ltd
A Division of the Carlton Publishing Group
20 Mortimer Street
London W1T 3JW

A CIP catalogue for this book is available from the British Library.

ISBN 978 1 78097 435 4

Printed in China

EROTIC

Dots

**JOIN THE DOTS TO CREATE
60 SEXY AND EXCITING PICTURES**

**CARLTON
BOOKS**

INTRODUCTION

In need of some raunchy entertainment to give you a lift? *Erotic Dots* will provide you with the ultimate in fun and excitement – or at least put a smile on your face. Arm yourself with a pen, and these sexy dot-todot pictures will be at the mercy of your artistic technique. Join the dots with a soft stroke or a swift flourish and watch the steamy positions take shape. So 1, 2, 3, and off you go..

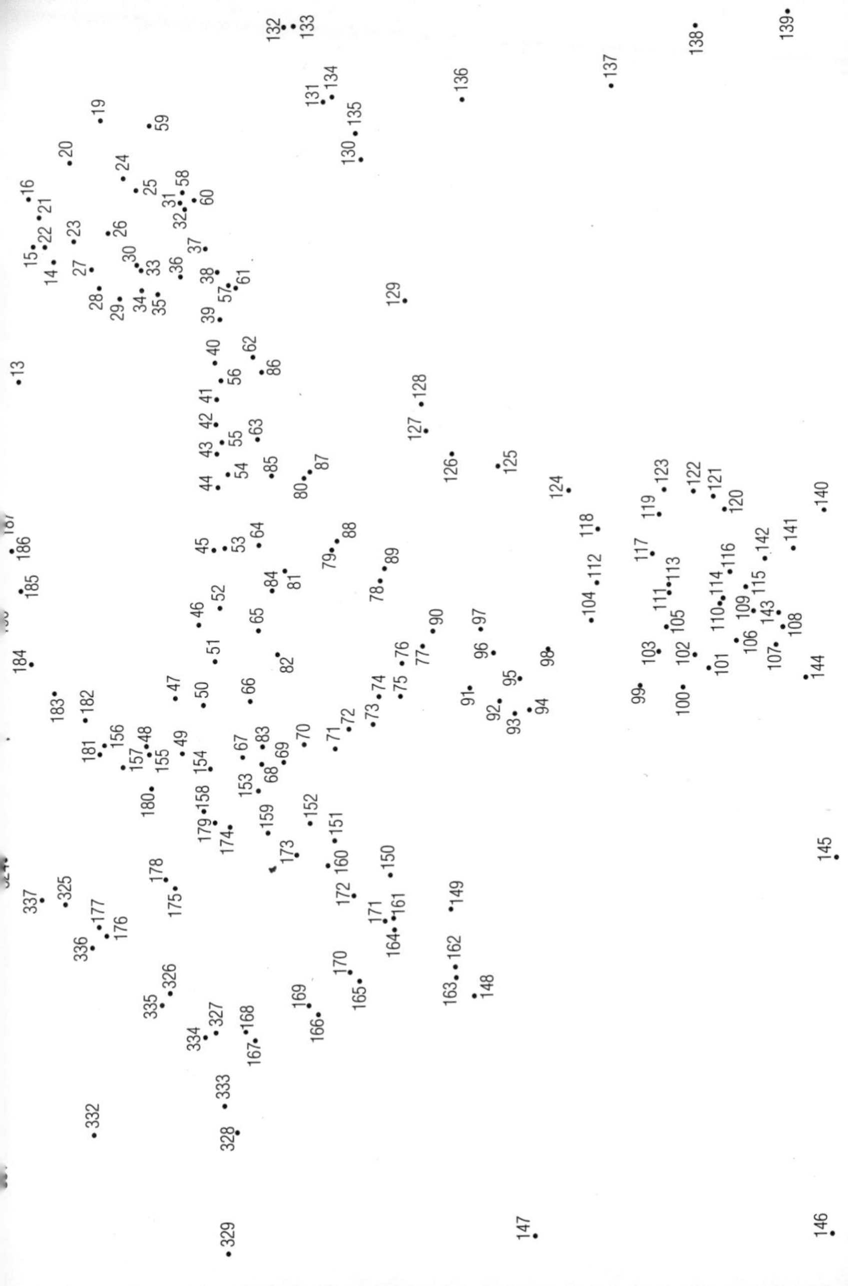

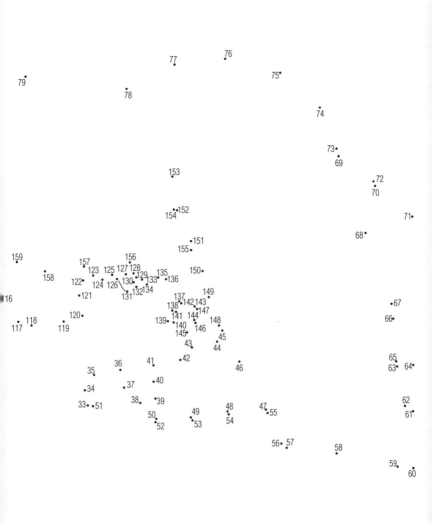

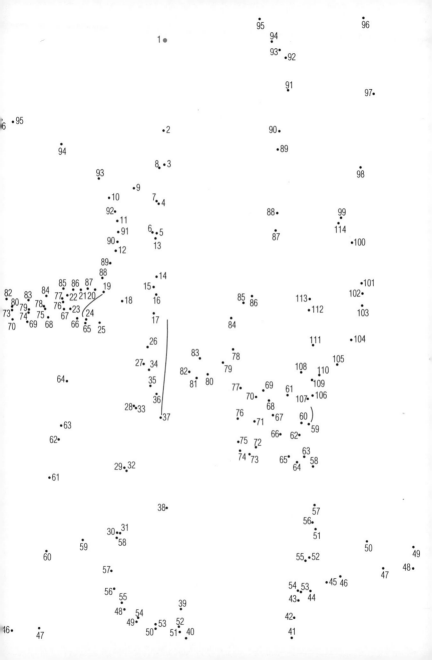

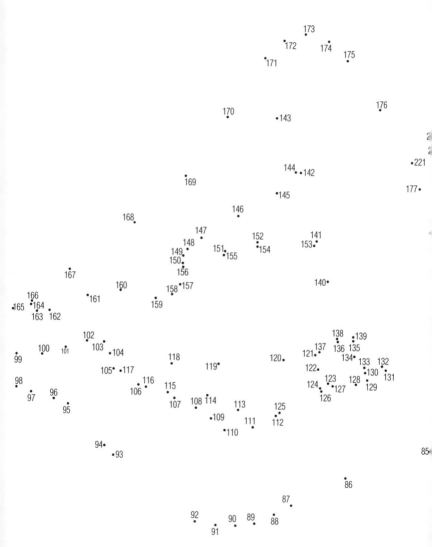

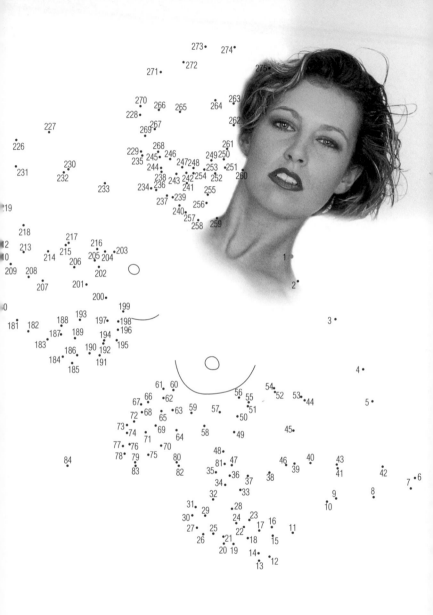

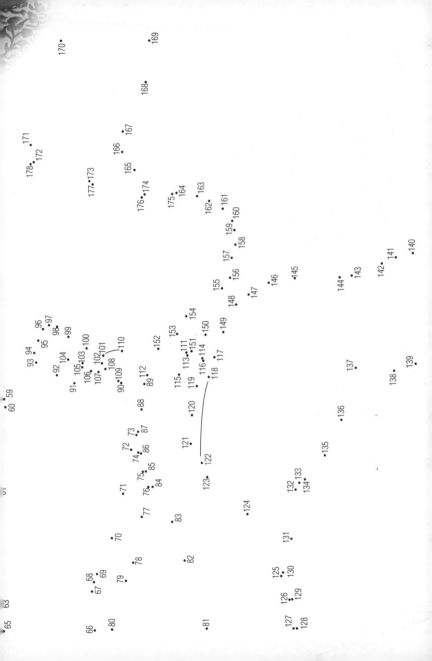

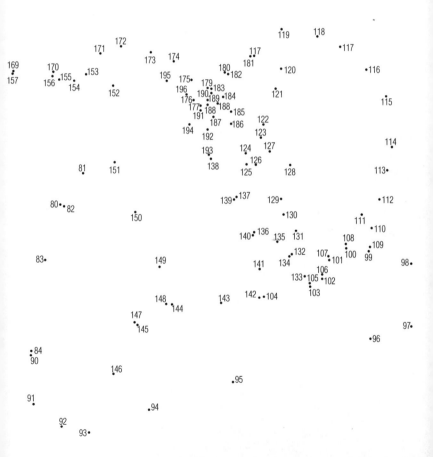

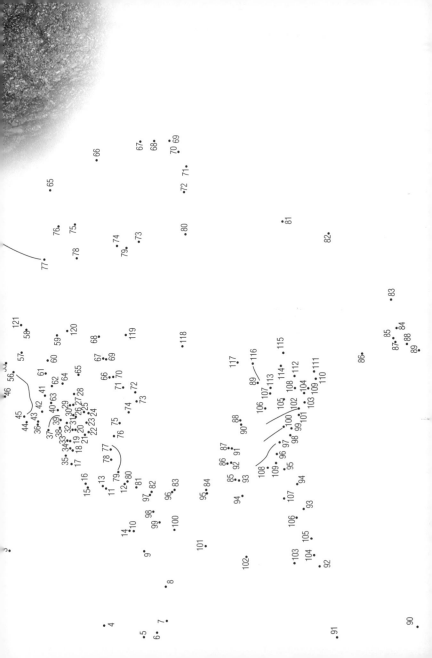

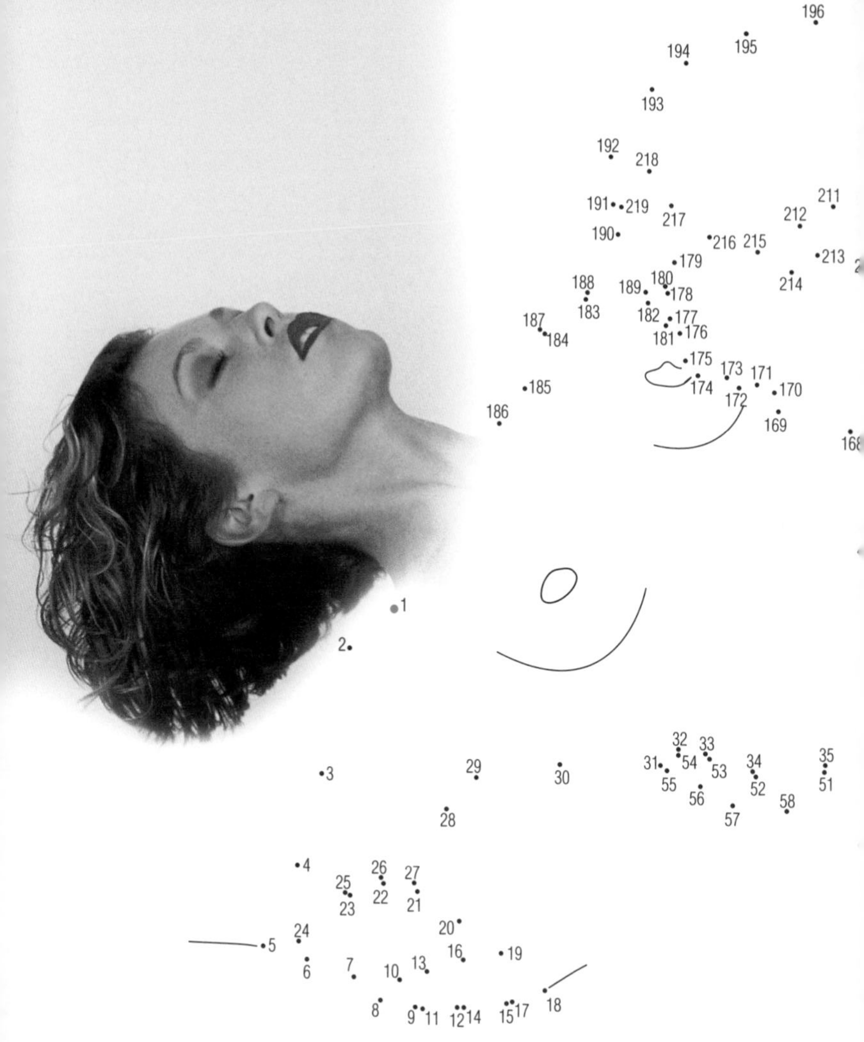

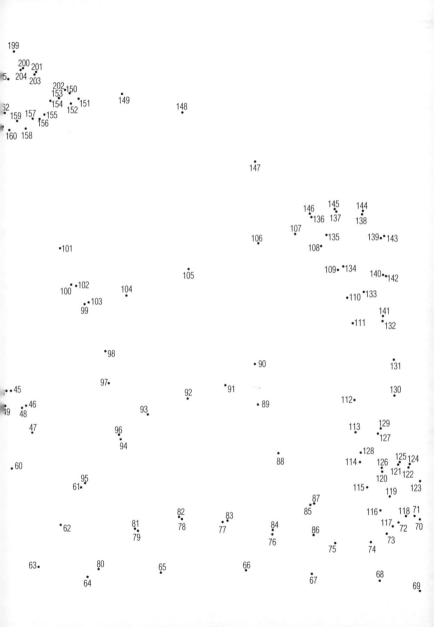

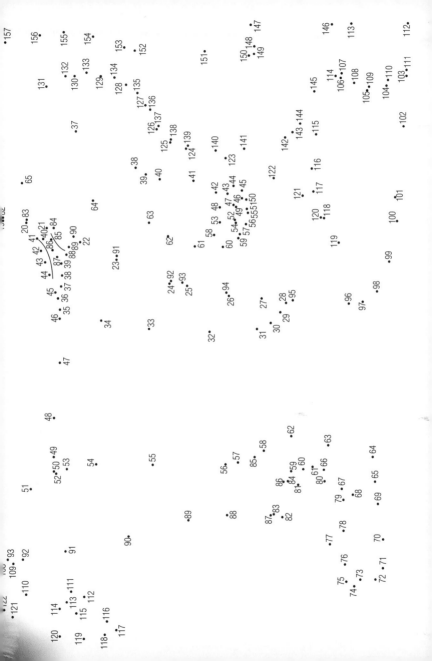

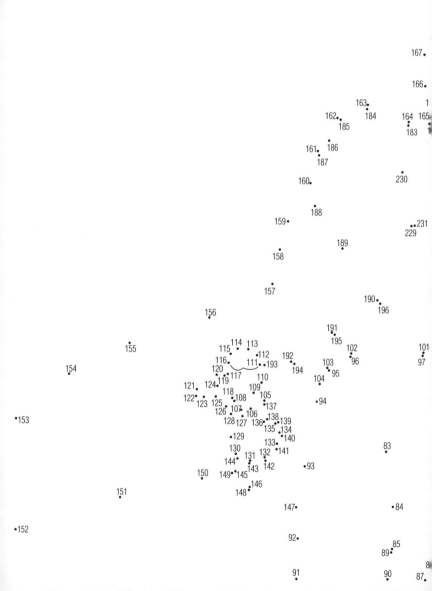

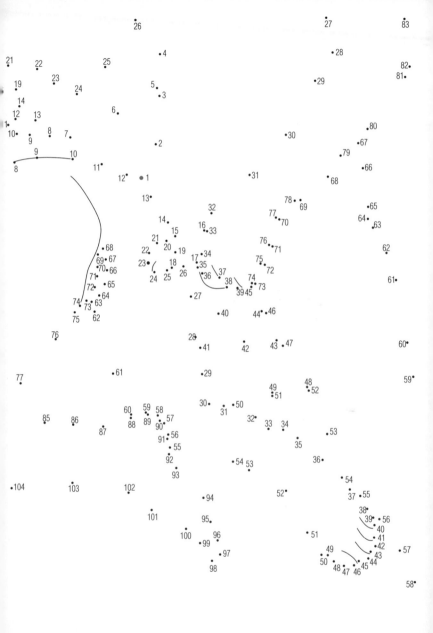

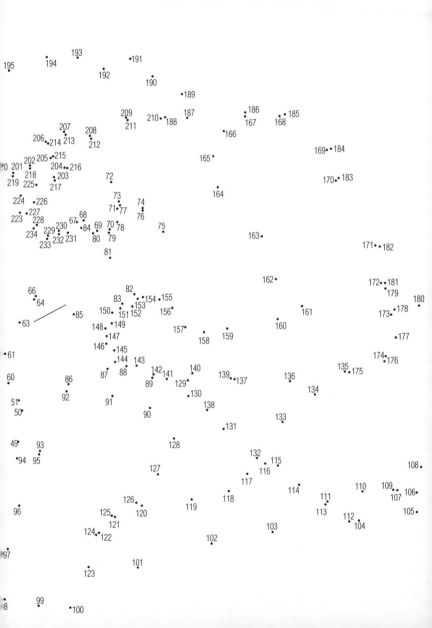

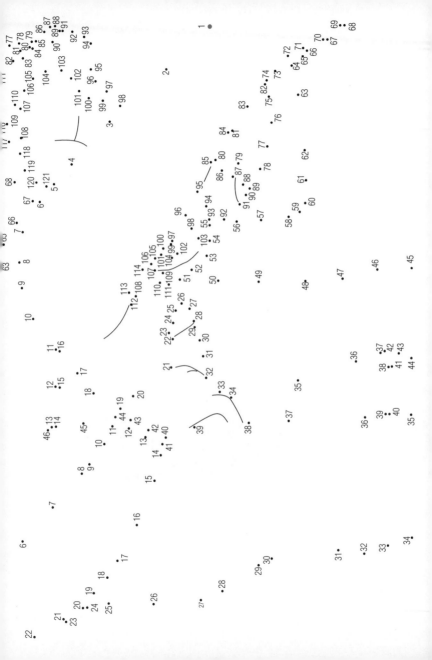

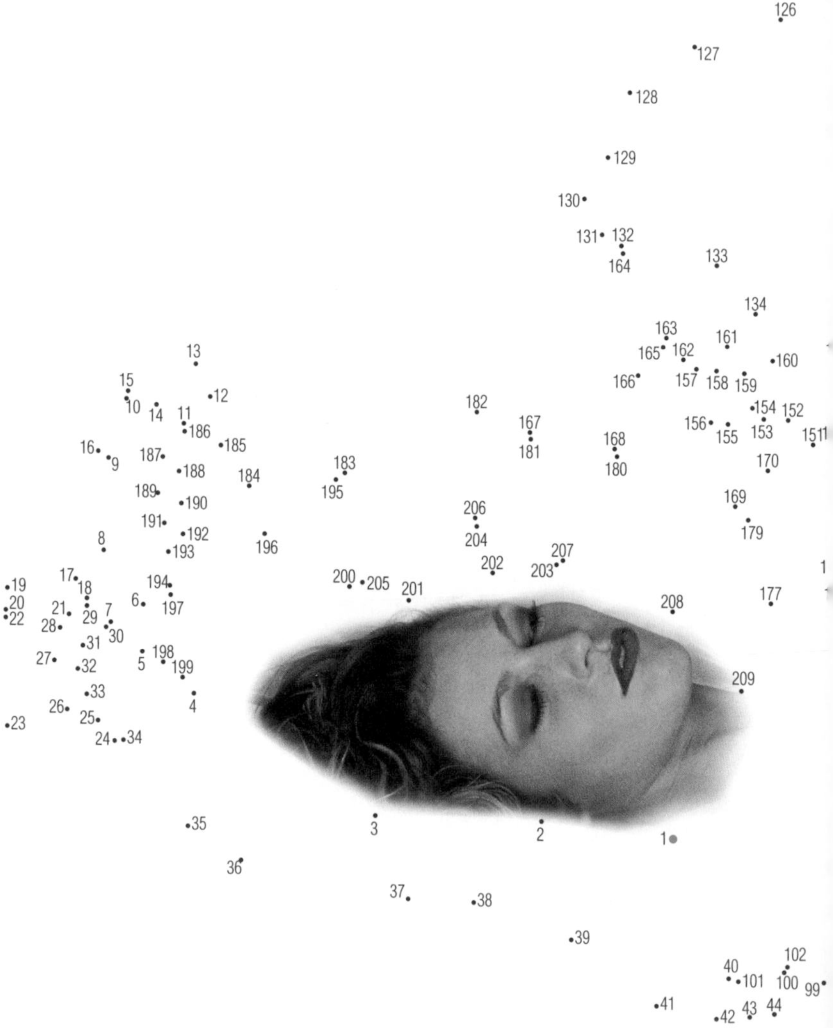

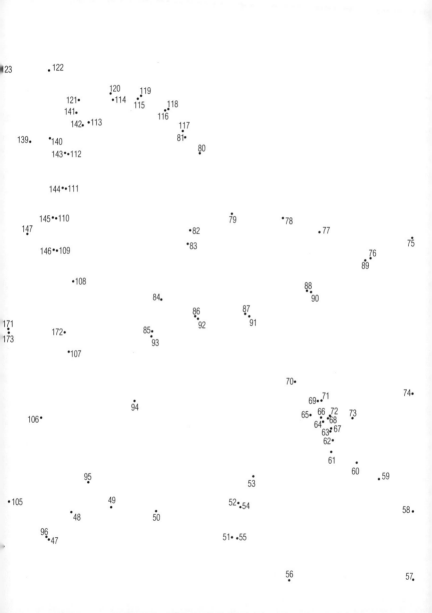

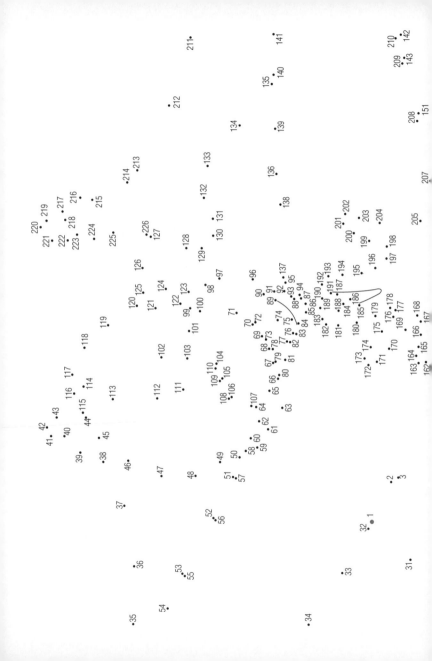

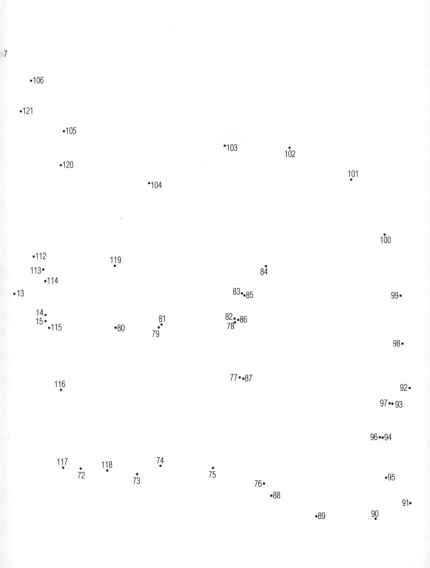

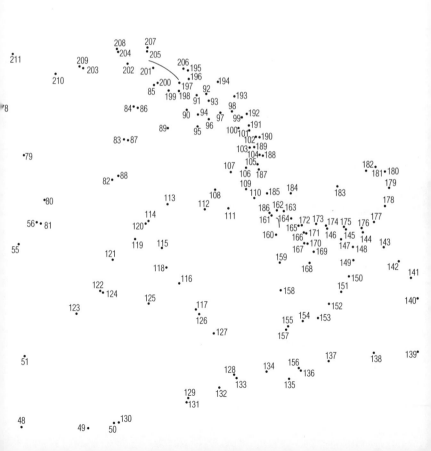

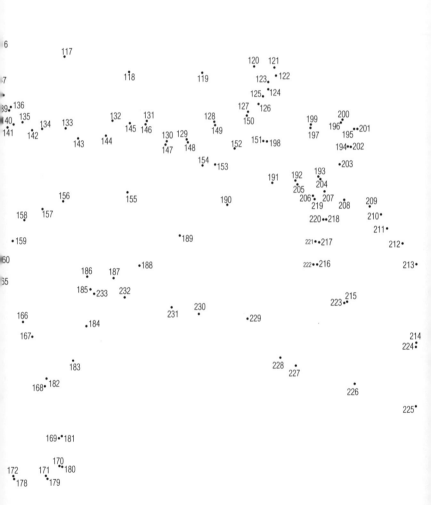

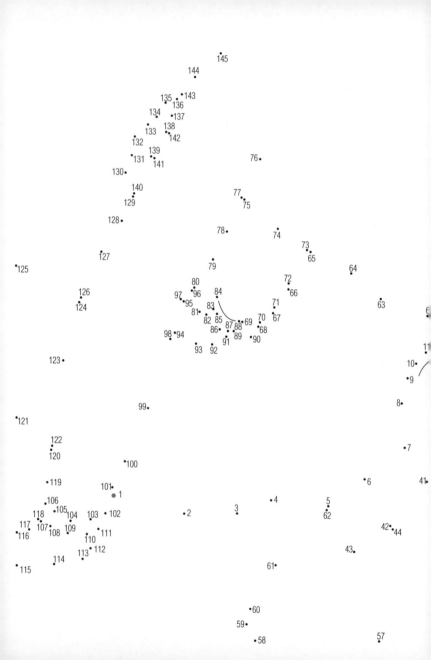

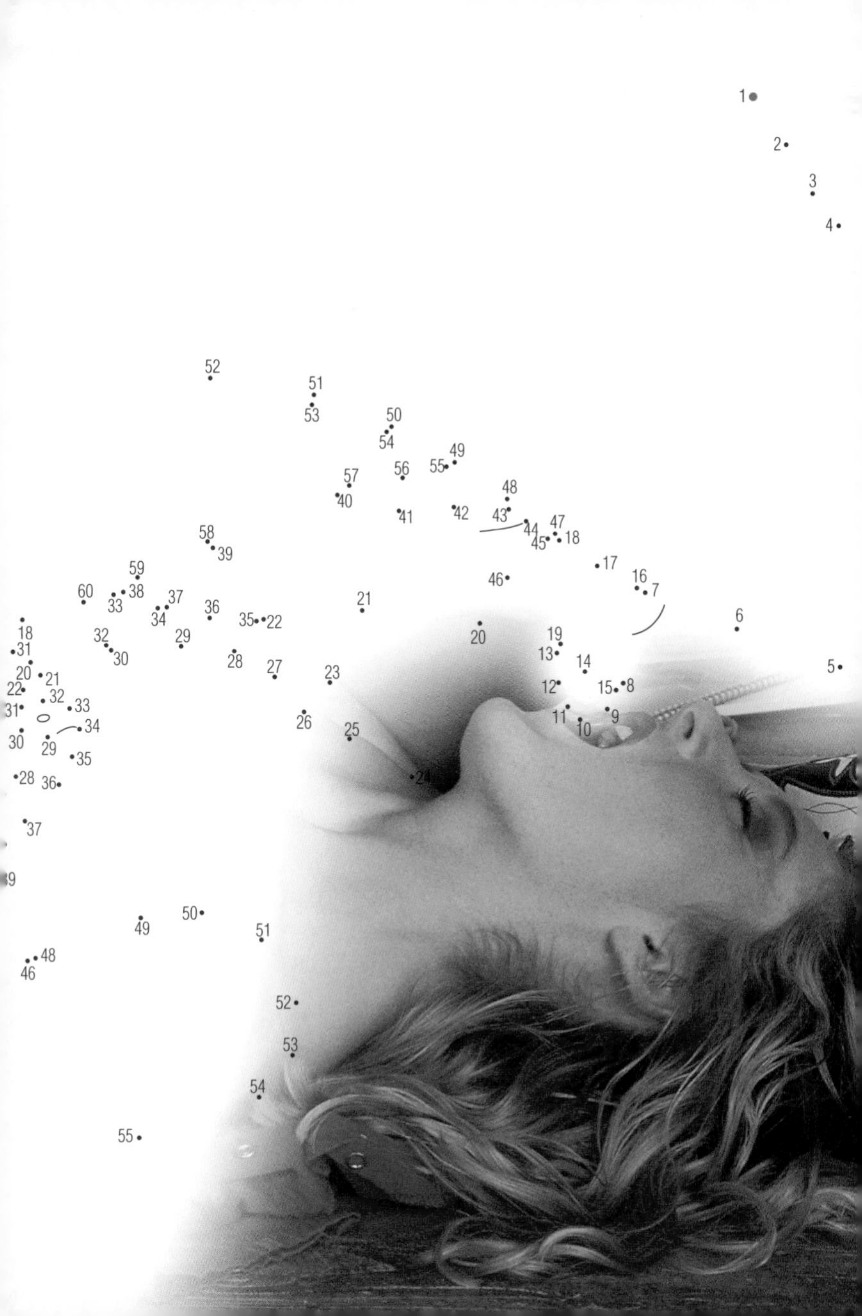

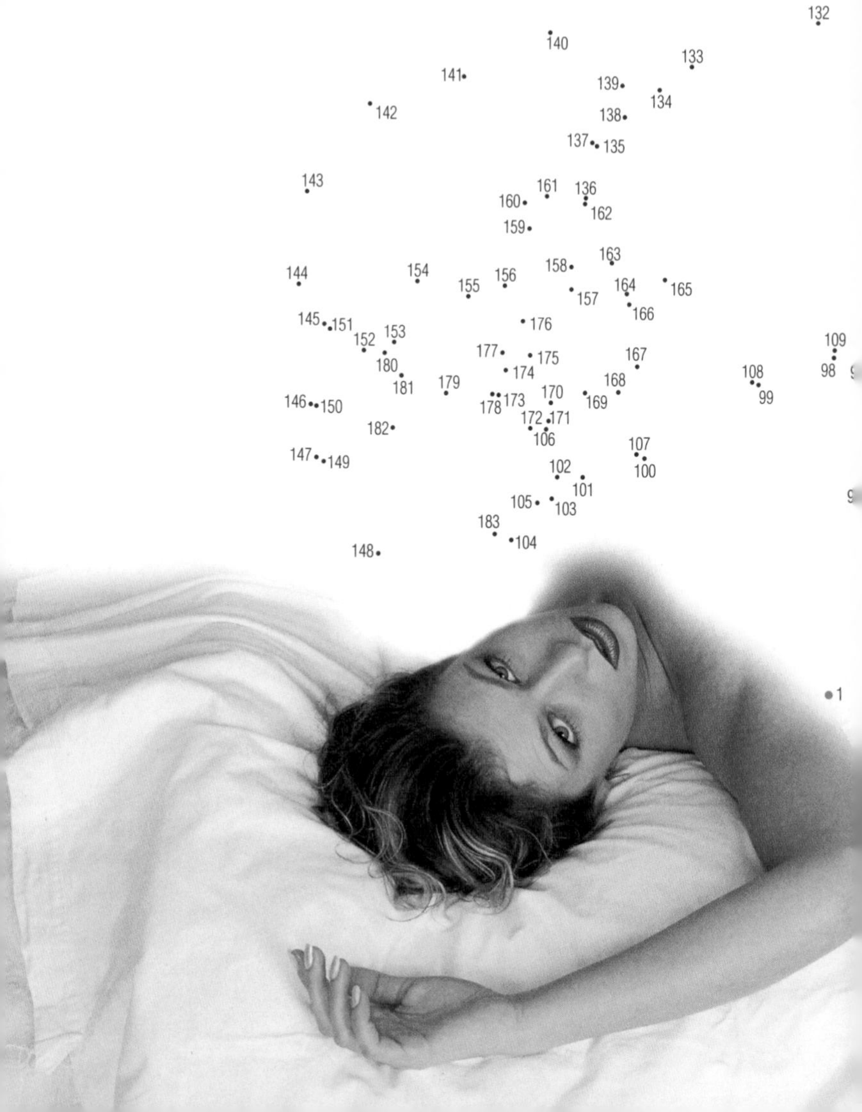

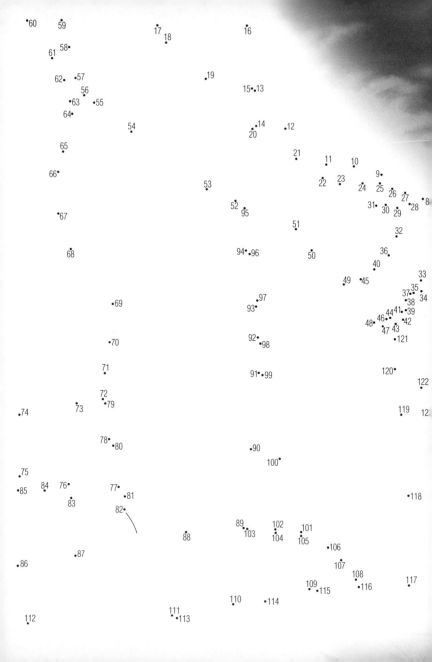

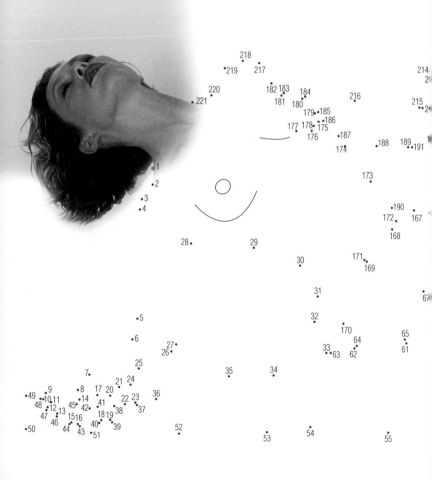

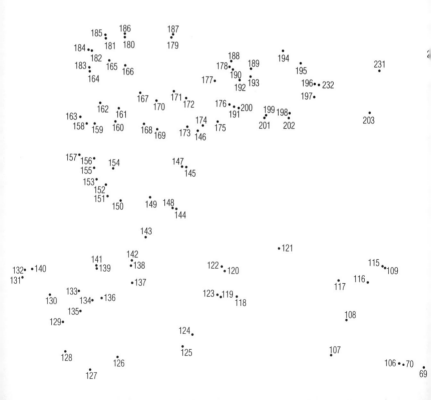

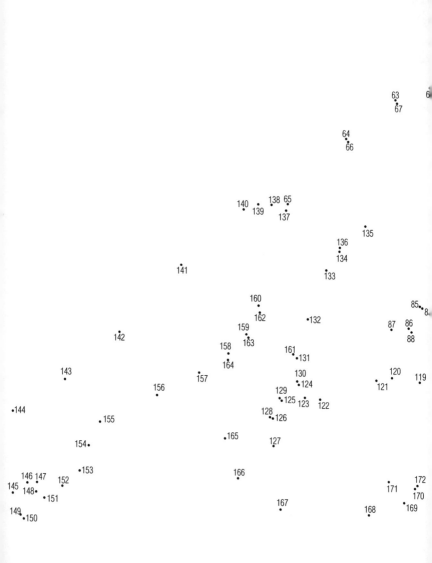

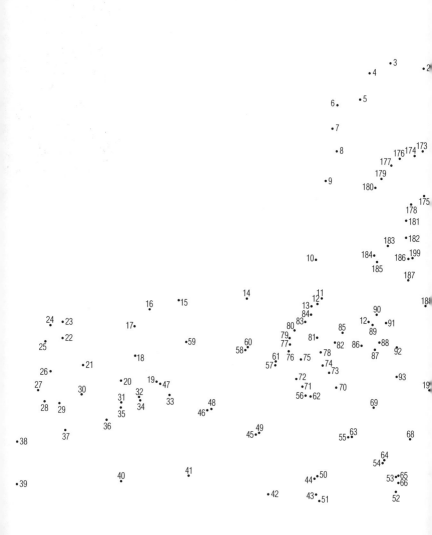

•157 •156

58

•155

160
  •162

•154

•163

•164   •153

•166

•165
205

196•202

195 203

•152
226

•151

193   204   216• 143 144   •150
      194•   215 142
           206• 210•   214
192   207 208 209   141 •145 •149
                    211   213   146   136   134
                    212 140 •148 137   135 •133   132
                                                130••120 131• •119

•95   129••121   118•
                                                              117•
•96   •97   •98   •99   128••122   116•

                                          127••123

•101 126••124   115•
      125   •113   •114

6
  105
8 109

104   103
110   111

102••112

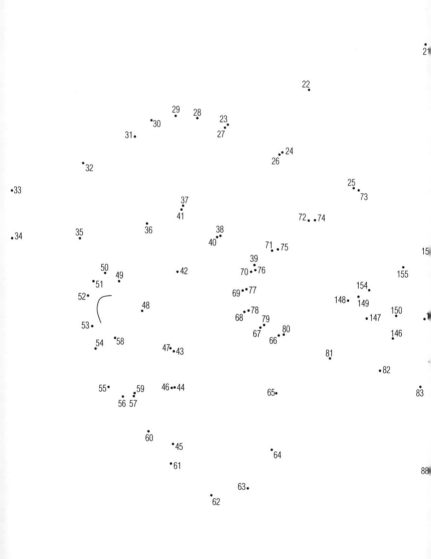

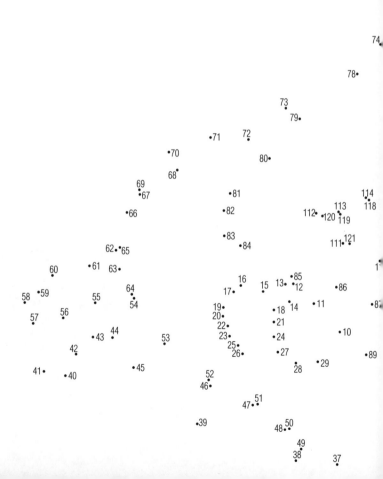

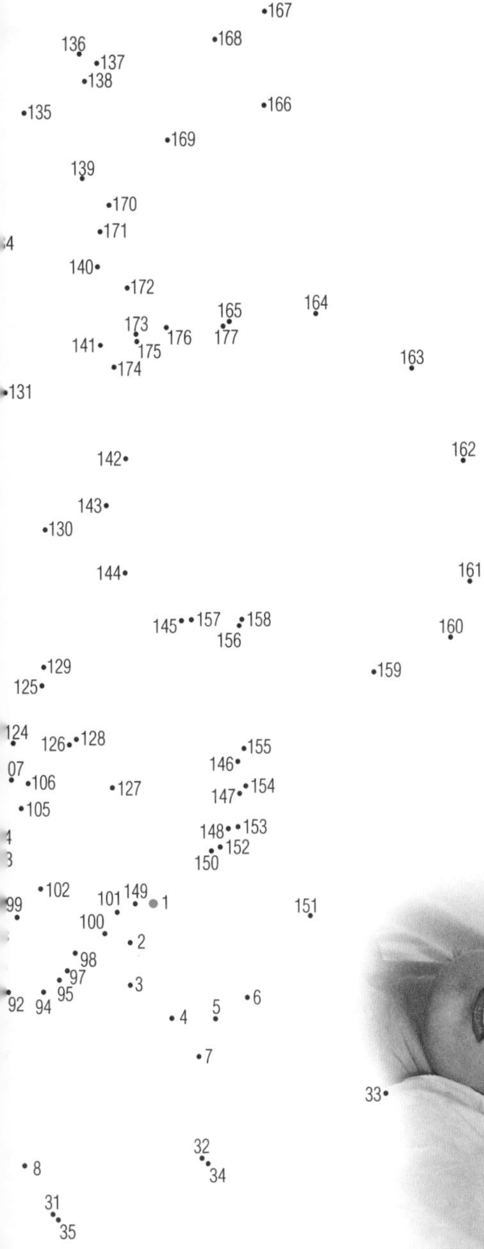
167
136
168
137
138
135
166
169
139
170
171
4
140
172
164
165
173
176
177
141
175
163
174
131
162
142
143
130
144
161
145
157
158
156
160
129
159
125
124
126
128
155
146
07
106
127
147
154
105
148
153
4
152
150
3
102
149
101
1
151
99
100
2
98
97
3
92
94
95
6
4
5
7
33
32
34
8
31
35

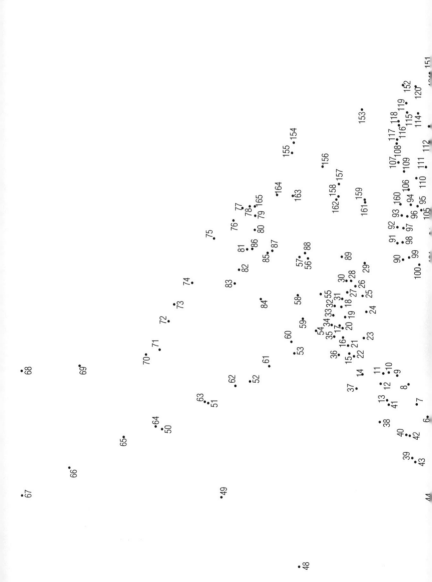

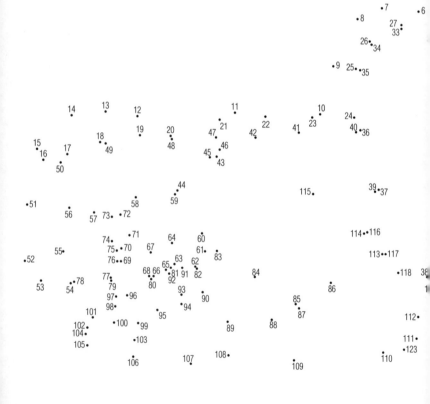

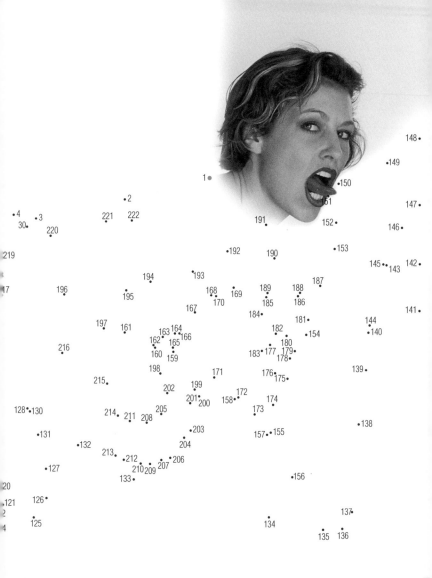

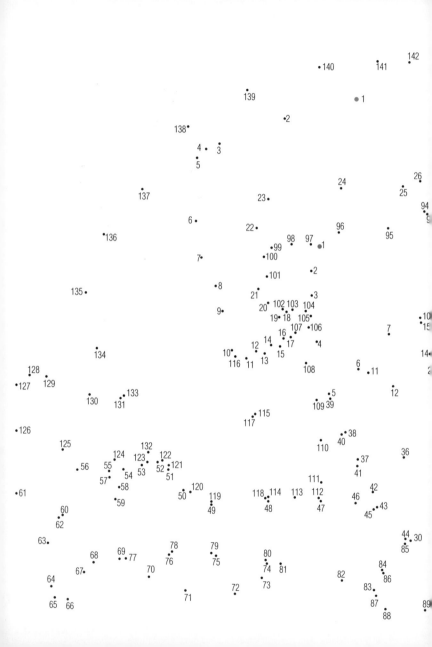

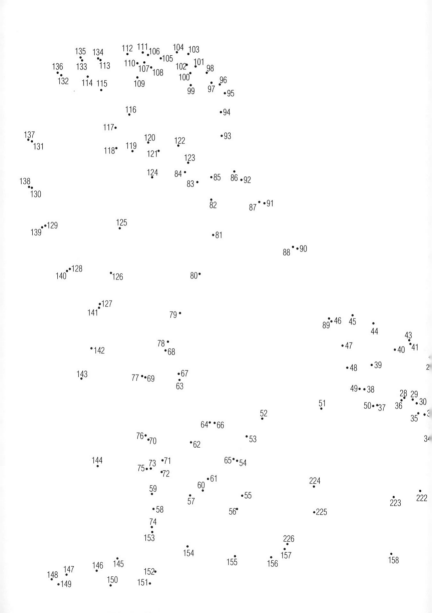

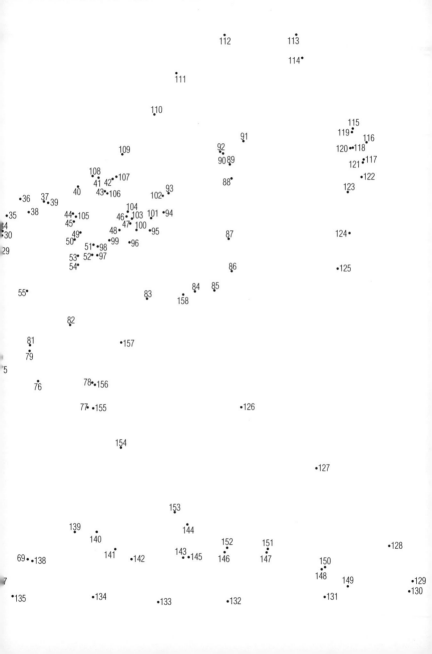

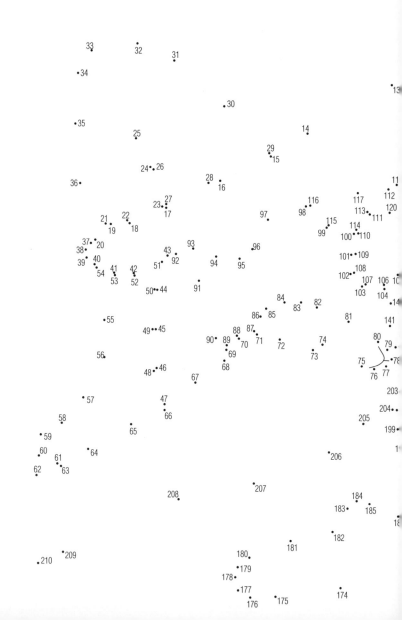

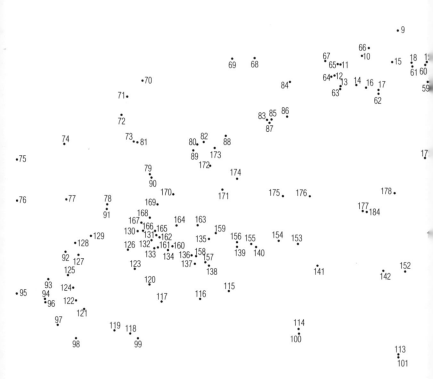

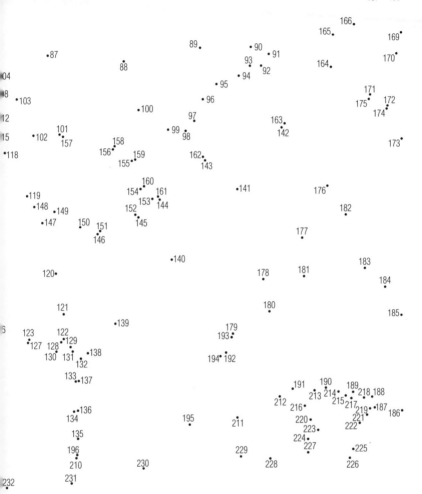

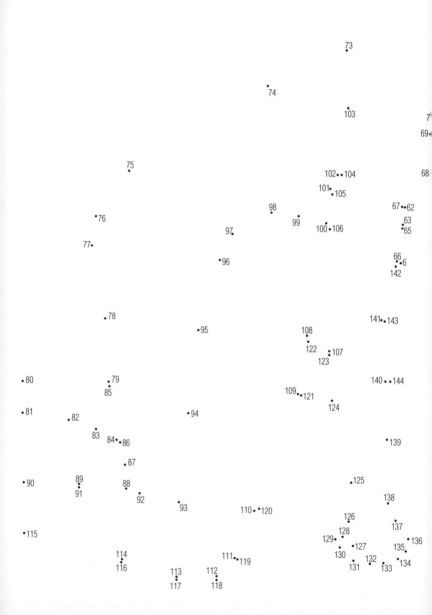

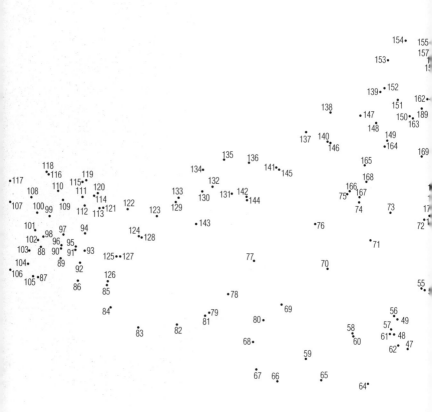

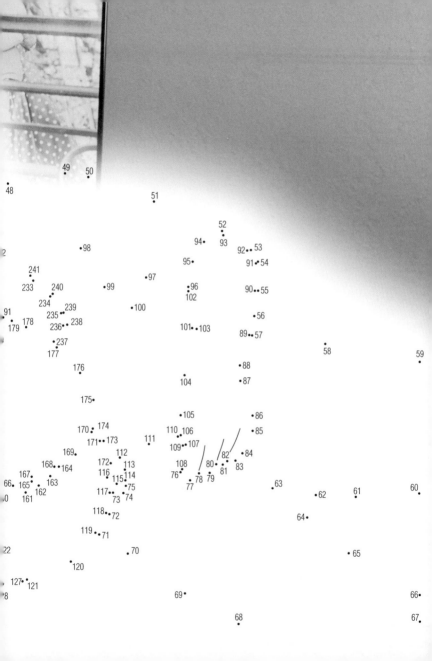

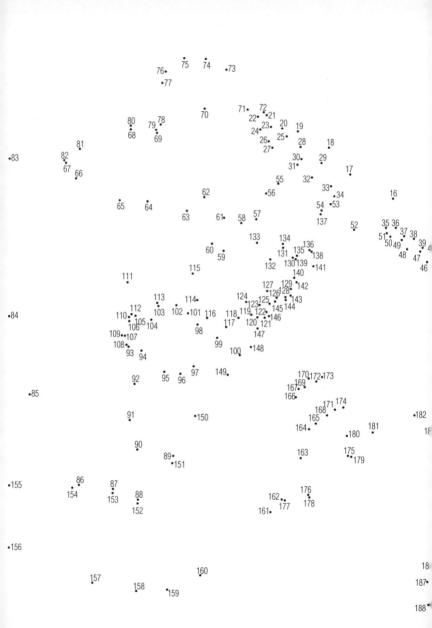

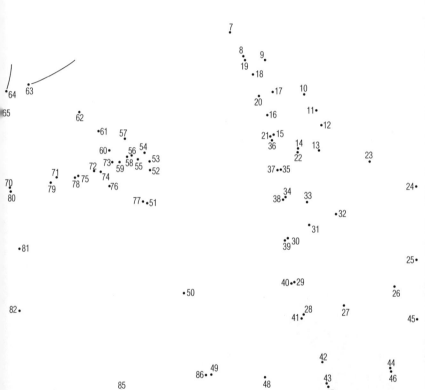

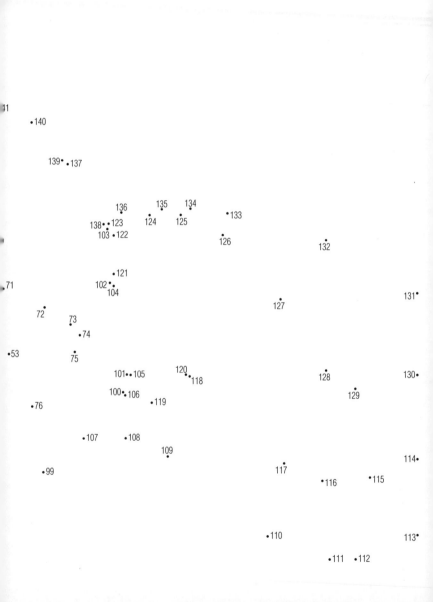

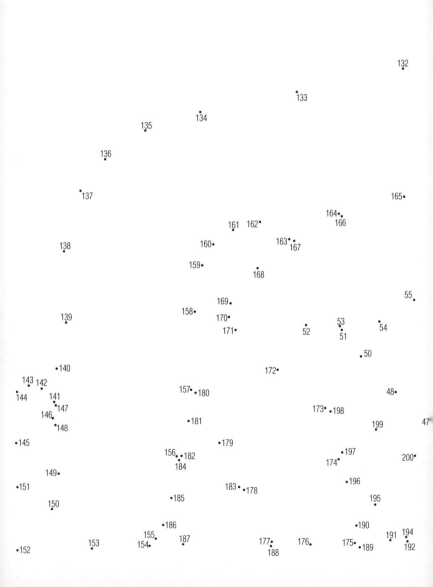

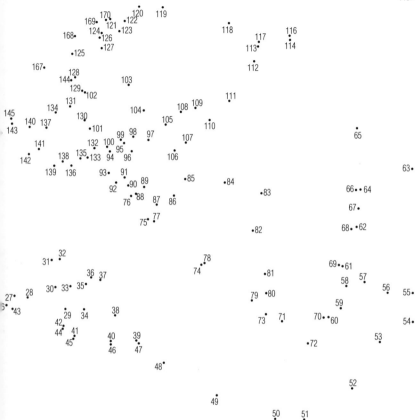

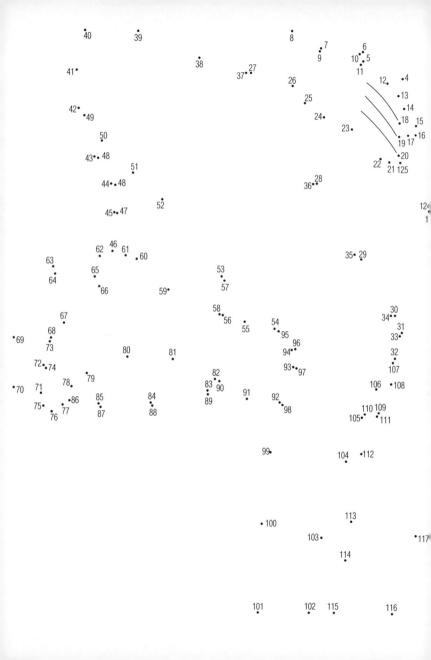

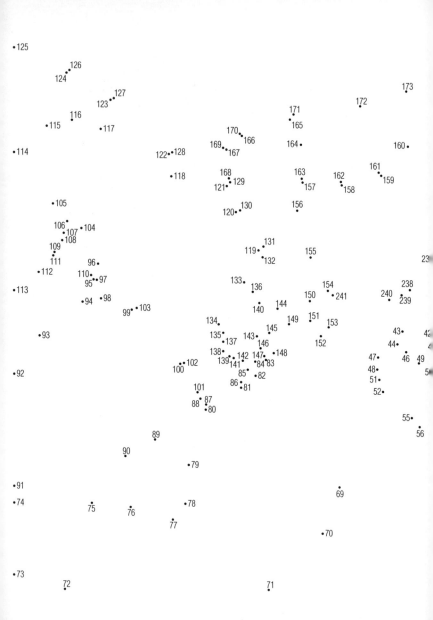

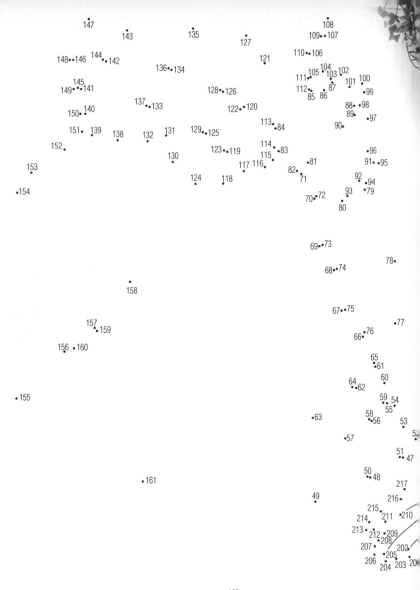

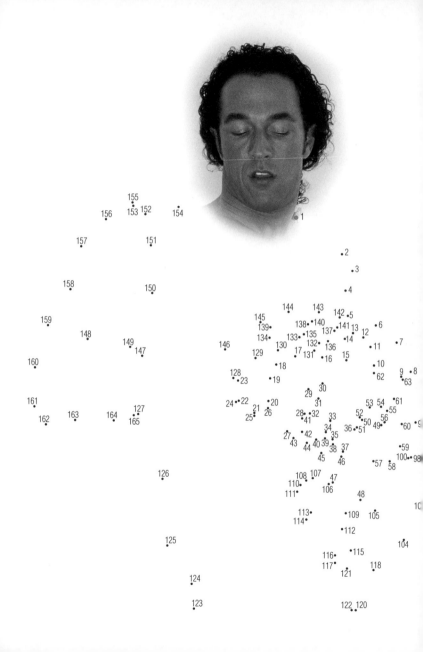

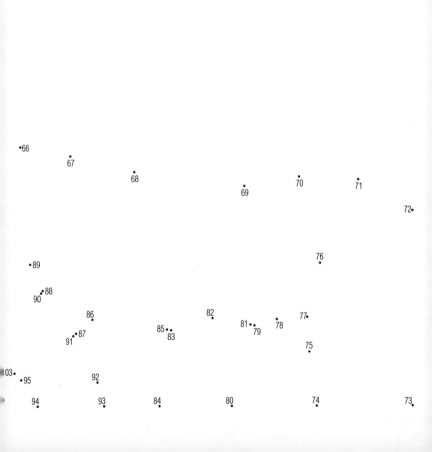

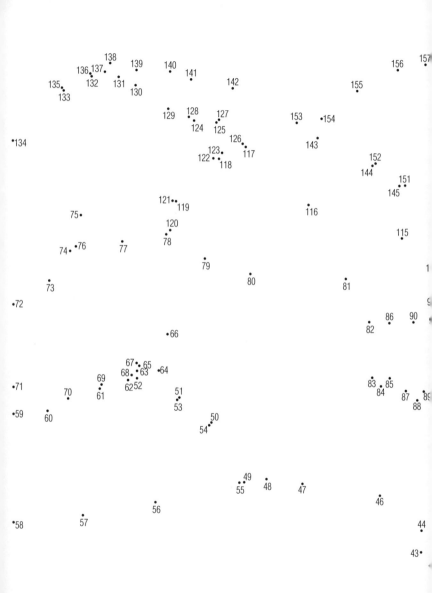

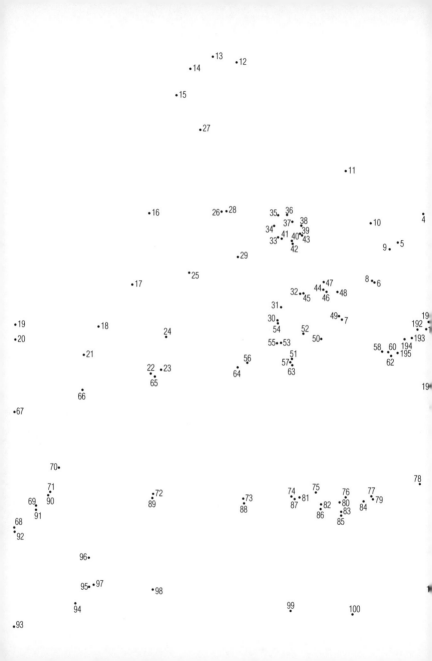

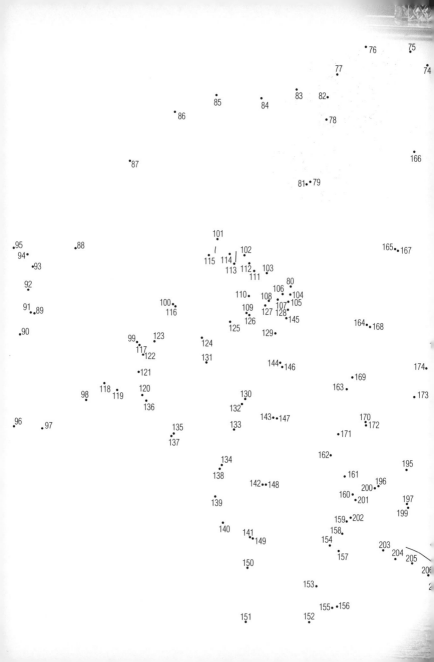

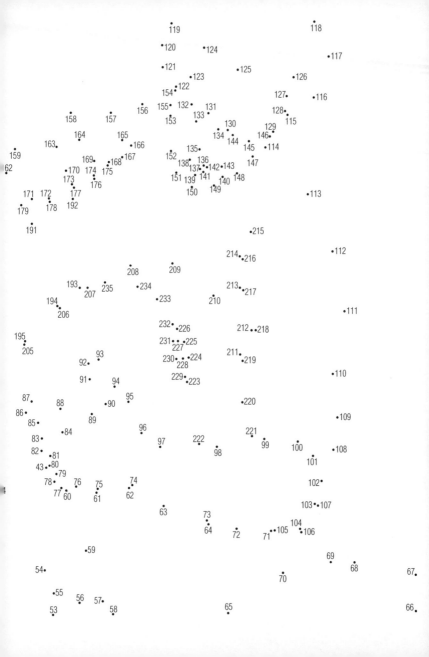

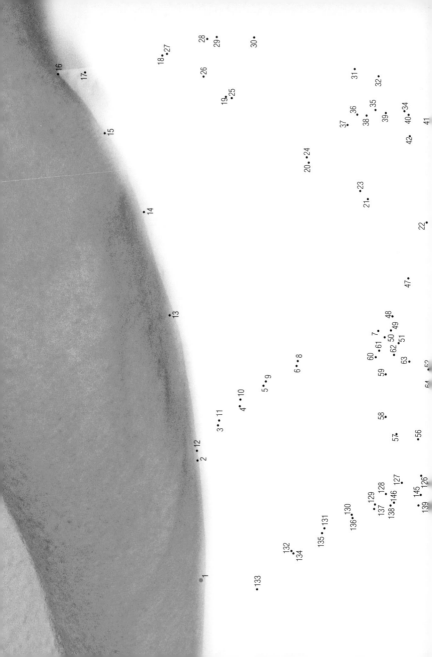

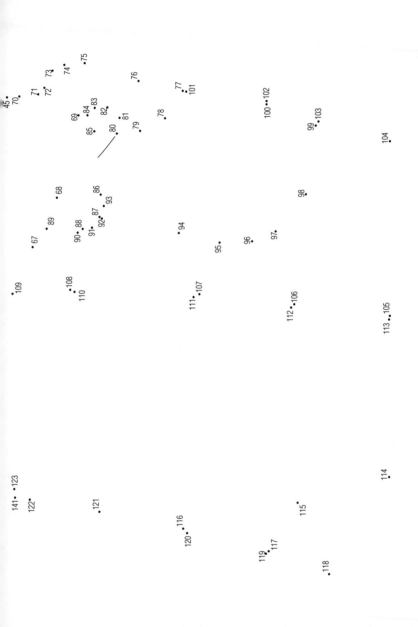

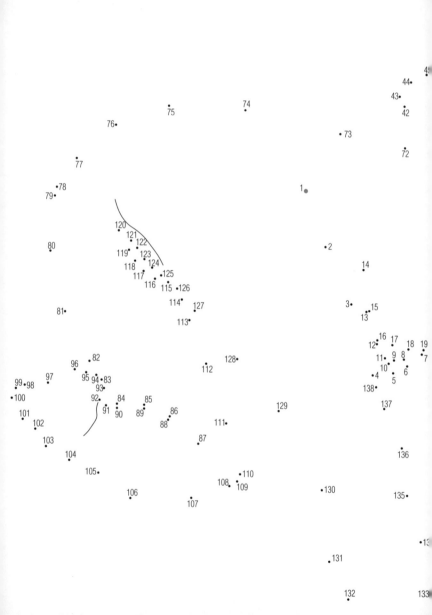

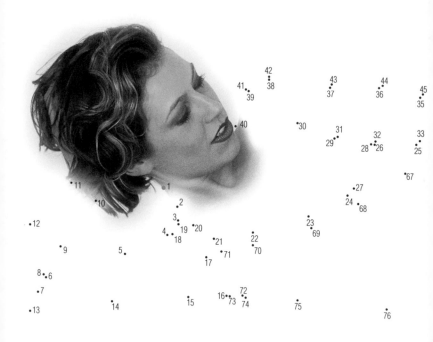

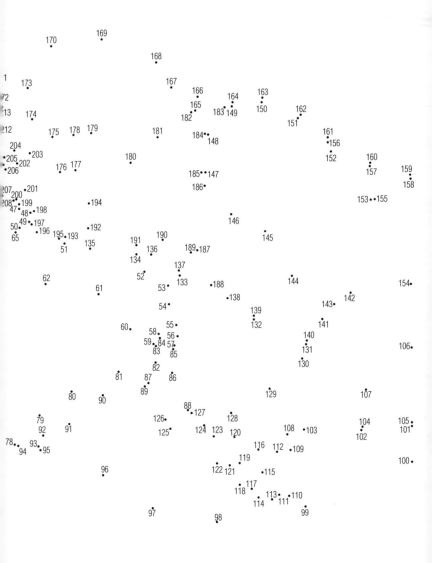

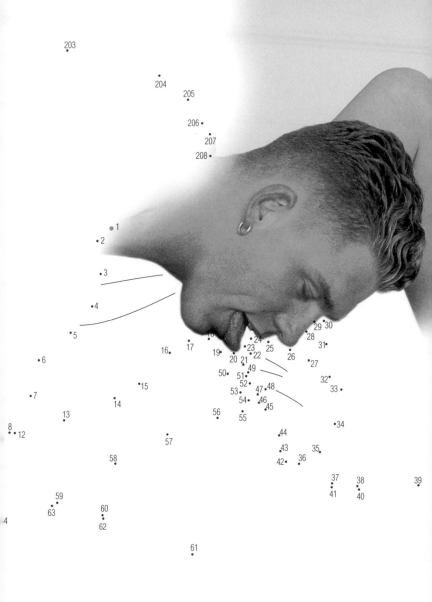

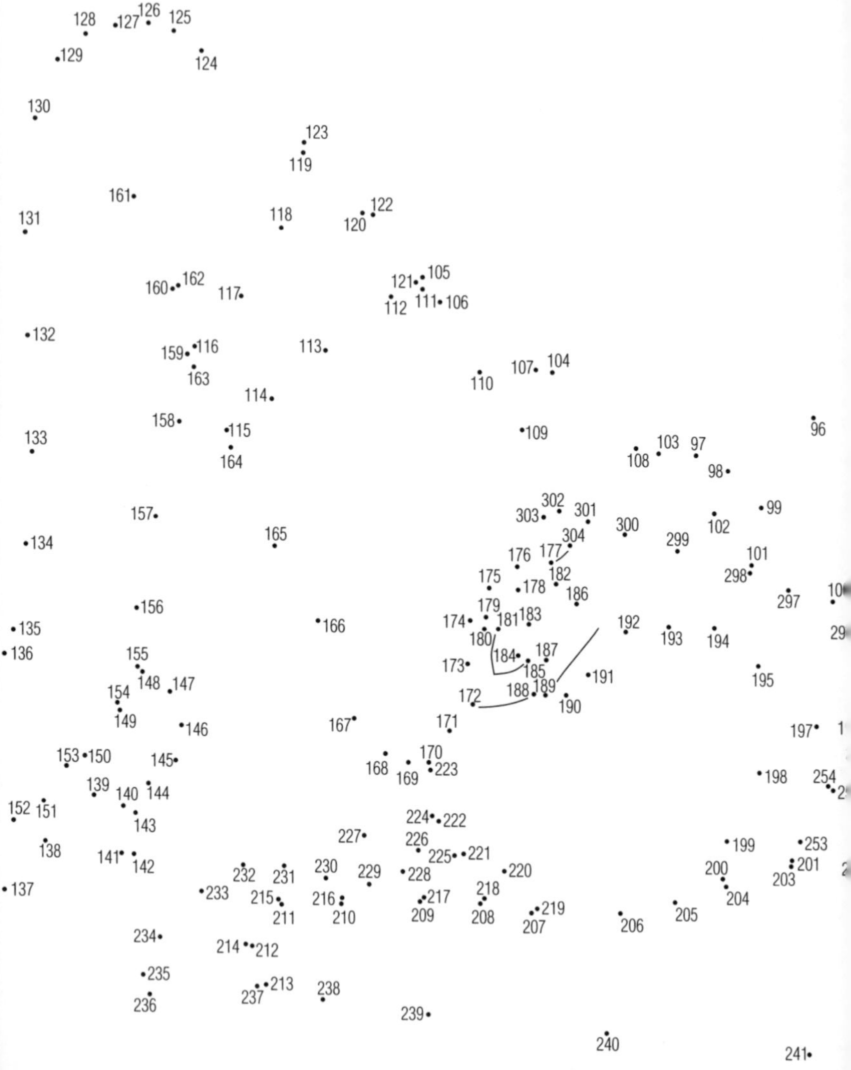

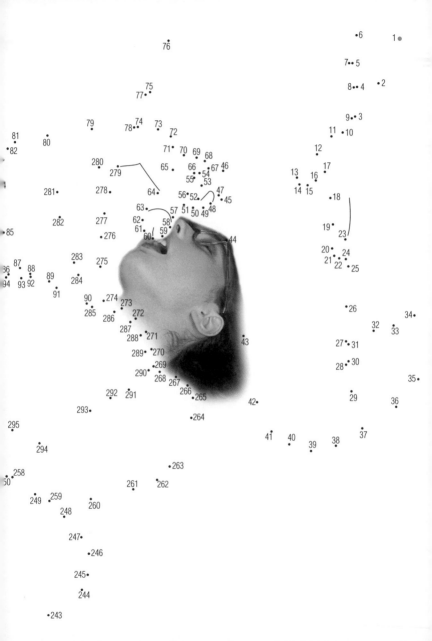

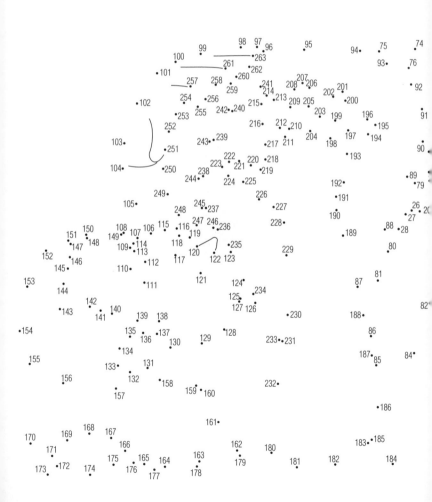